There is a Case That I ∀m

torrin a. greathouse

Therə is a Case That I ∀m
Copyright © 2017 torrin a. greathouse

Published by Damaged Goods Press
Edited by Caseyrenée Lopez
www.damagedgoodspress.com

All rights reserved. No part or parts of this book may be reproduced in any format without the expressed written consent of Damaged Goods Press or torrin a. greathouse.

ISBN-13: 978-0997826753
ISBN-10: 0997826754

Printed in the United States of America
Petersburg, Virginia

Cover Design by Justine Alldredge and Stephanie Cui

acknowledgements

My gratitude to the editors of the publications in which these poems originally appeared, sometimes in earlier versions:

"The First-Time I Was Catcalled" first appeared in *The Feminist Wire*
"Gender of the Day" first appeared in *One Sentence Poems*
"Nonbinary Logic," "Three Queers in a Car in America," "Jaz Told Me to Write a Poem About the Things I Fear Putting into Words," & "When My Partner Writes" first appeared in *Crab Fat Magazine*
"Bar Joke" first appeared in *Cadence Collective*
"Drag" first appeared in *Rabbit Catastrophe Review*
"The House of Walls," "Ode to Laura Jane Grace," & "Ending in a Fistful of Ash" first appeared in *Yellow Chair Review*
"To the People Who Call Me Brave," & "True[*]" first appeared in *Seafoam Magazine*
"Calloused Hands" first appeared in *Moonsick Magazine*
"On the Midnight Sky," & "Fireworks Calling to Us Like a Mother in the Distance" first appeared in *Glass - A Journal of Poetry*
"Panic Attack as a Four-Part Word Problem" first appeared in *Rust+Moth*
"Unfinished Scenes," & "Aubade [From Body to Little Black Dress]" first appeared in *Emerge Literary Journal*
"The Uncertainty Principle," & "If/Then or An Open Letter to High School GSAs" first appeared in *Calamus Journal*

I want to briefly thank *Winter Tangerine Review*, whose workshops helped produce many of these poems, as well as my loving partner Canelle, who edited many of them. I also want to extend my greatest thanks to *Crab Fat Magazine* and Damaged Goods Press for always believing in my work.

Therə is a Case That I ∀m

poems
torrin a. greathouse

contents

9   Nonbinary Logic or ∃x
11   True[*]
13   Gender of the Day
14   On Driving Home from the Bar, Springsteen Playing Again
16   Bar Joke
17   The First-Time I was Catcalled
18   The Uncertainty Principle
19   Drag
20   Gender of the Day
21   Three Queers in a Car in America
22   The House of Walls
24   To the People Who Call Me Brave
25   Jaz Told Me to Write a Poem About the Things I Fear Putting into Words
27   On the Midnight Sky, Fireworks Calling to Us Like a Mother in the Distance
29   Panic Attack as a Four-Part Word Problem
30   Gender of the Day
31   Unfinished Scenes
33   Calloused Hands
35   When My Partner Writes
36   Gender of the Day
37   Aubade [From Body to Little Black Dress]
39   If/Then or An Open Letter to High School GSAs
41   Ode to Laura Jane Grace, Ending in a Fistful of Ash
43   Gender of the Day
44   The Principle of Explosion

about torrin a. greathouse

Nonbinary Logic or $\exists x$

> "What separates poetry from other language is that it cannot be reduced to logic."
> -Sean Walsh

B = boy | G = girl | X = me

$X (\neg B) \land (\neg G) \Rightarrow X \equiv ?$
    if i am not boy & not girl,
    what am I defined as? what value do I hold?

$X (B \land \neg B) \lor (G \land \neg G) \Rightarrow X \equiv 0$
    if i am boy & not boy
        or girl & not girl,
                      then this body is nothing.
                  it is outside operational definitions.
it cannot exist.
i do not exist.
    i am not a person,
        but a ghost to this logic.

$\forall x (Bx \lor Gx) \therefore 0$
    for all versions of a person like me,
i must be boy or girl   therefore / nothing.

there are no inbetweens in this logic, only violent lines & the red that pools beneath / solutions this logic sees / only as mistakes.

according to this logic

$\neg \exists x ((Bx \land \neg Bx) \lor \quad (G \land \neg Gx))$
    there is no case where i can be   / boy & not boy
                              or girl & not girl.

where i am more than the bear trap
    of my body, where my genitals ≠ me,
        where my brain is more than just
            passenger in car driving off of

cliff.

given that $\forall x\, (Bx \lor Gx)$ is true
& $(\forall x\, (Bx \lor Gx)) \Rightarrow (\neg \exists x((Bx \land \neg Bx) \lor (G \land \neg Gx)))$

solve for a version of this world
      where X belongs.

True[*]

i sit in bed / the only place i sit like this /
bra stolen from the summer girl
wrapped tight as a belt
          [the bible belt?]
around my chest / wishing this cotton
looked like flesh.

              knowing it doesn't.

i wonder if this is how my boyfriend's binder
makes him feel / guilt begins /
to flow like blood.

i have grown accustomed to this / rusty lipped guilt /
thoughts that taste like every beating
i have ever avoided.

i want to take a razor to this traitor /
      beard across my face
[dig past the hairs to my skin / paint it like my lips.]

every time i sing the word true
in tune with Laura's pain
it feels like biting my tongue
i wish i could watch the blood / splatter into the sink.

          a perfect bloody asterix.

like me.
    an exception.
    [just invisible / enough.]

it's not that i don't want people to see,
but i remember how it feels / not to eat,
& guilt goes down easier / with wine.

i never intended to hide,

i would love to walk a mile in her shoes
but they don't come in my size,
    & i couldn't afford them anyway
            [not in this economy]

Gender of the Day

a lake opening up,
    water cresting like teeth / to swallow a boat
like the way a mouth opens up
    only to swallow / its words

the way they can make my breath
    into shipwrecks / on the crags of my jaw
how easily an angry voice
    like so much thunder / ˙on the tongue

can turn my throat into a flooded graveyard
where no words surface / as identifiable remains

On Driving Home from the Bar, Springsteen Playing Again

> *"I check my look in the mirror / I wanna change my clothes, my hair my face."*
> -Bruce Springsteen, "Dancing in the Dark"

here we are again Bruce.
    seems like you & me,
  we're always heading somewhere else.

                            born for riding engines
                      into the grave, 10,000 horses
                                broken in unison.
gas tank's half empty
       & you're singing out the same old song.

i wonder what you imagined there,
       dancing in the dark,
the light of a candle's flame
    or a body like mine, bra on breastless chest,
       [in bed   alone]

both so easily snuffed out for
mocking nature & its rigid lines.

i wonder what you meant when you said
you wanted to change your face,
                      when you looked in the mirror
                            did you feel the same
                                    as i do?

Roy's fingers fistfight ivory
while my mind wanders to the girl in the bar
      [on the corner of Almond & Glassel]

                    varsity jacket,
                hair cropped short
        around the amaretto curves of her face,

i find myself wishing i looked like her,
        wondering if she wishes she looked just like you.

i wonder what you were looking for
in the mirror, what face you wanted to see
    staring back,
            & what you would think about these words
                    meaning so much to a kid like me?

Bar Joke

a man & a woman walk into a bar / & sit on the same stool /
the man & the woman are the same person //

which is to say / a freak walks into a bar & sits down / grips their beer
bottle as tight as a weapon / presses it to their lips & wishes it were a
knife //

a freak walks into a bar & sits / clutching a bottle like a hand- grenade
/ & the whole room cracks their grins wide teeth into vultures beaks //

the freak reluctantly unroots their fingers / from the glass & slinks
across the room / for the bomb-shelter of a bathroom / hopes there is
only one //

which is to say / that hallways like this are always the most fucked up
form of let's make a deal / & the contestant is praying / to find less
violence behind door #1 //

which is to say / a person in a dress / with a cock / walks into men's
bathroom in a dive bar / on the cheap side of Santa Ana / & prays that
they no one decides to paint the linoleum / the same color as their lips

which is to say / that i am afraid whenever i go out / & some days
i am terrified to look like myself / & still leave my house //

which is to say / when i am in the clothes i feel most comfortable in / i
cannot tell if it is the tightness of my shirt / or the fear / that is keeping
the air from my lungs //

which is to say / i see everything around me like a knife / every
doorway a weapon / every sharp corner another place / that someone
could make a stain of me //

which is to say / i am afraid of disappearing by morning //
people like me / which is to say / freaks / walk out their door
in the morning / & into the guillotine's waiting mouth //

The First-Time I was Catcalled

i was catcalled   as a girl //
six-foot-tall / size two skinny jeans / cut tourniquet tight /
against my slender frame / & hair hanging down
past the curve of my waist / how could he be blamed? //

when i turned around [foolish enough to smile]
he proved his masculinity was only as fragile / as my boy face
lip split / canyon wide / blood making a halo on each of my teeth /
making rivers over my chin / & Rorschach on the concrete //

school security looking the other way /
for the first time / i understood why women are so afraid //

after all / wasn't i asking for it? /
dressing up like a target   or a woman /
as if to him they were any different //

before i was the boy he beat / like a side of beef /
hung from a warehouse ceiling / i was just another
piece of meat / to be consumed //

i still remember looking up at his face / the way his lips curved /
up at the edges like a meat hook / the way his eyes
flourished like a swarm of flies / at the scent of blood //

it took me years / to put back on these clothes /
to call myself anything but him / to undress myself
of this borrowed wolves clothing //

it's so simple to forget / how easily i have become /
both meat & hook / deer & headlight / wolf & sheep //

but if you tell me that catcalling / is not an act of violence /
i will remind you that wolves howl / to signal their pack to prey //

The Uncertainty Principle

a cat is sealed in a steel box / poison is sealed in a glass vial / a hammer & a human chest both freeze / in time a second before the pulse / the pound the broken seal & air rushing out // a radioactive isotope is the only thing that holds / hammer from fall / the 50-50 odds that separate / a heartbeat from a body spilling out its heat / seeking homeostasis // the lid slams shut & the cat becomes / a blur of living & dead //

i walk into a bathroom & the door slams shut / i become / a blur of man & woman of living & dead // the uncertainty principle says that / until an event is observed it may / or may not / have occurred / a person stares at me / from across the room & my body / splits in two / body wrapped in Schrödinger's black dress / becomes a blur / while their mind strips me down / to hot skin / pulling back layers / tender like a butcher stripping a body / down to red meat //

the bathroom door slams shut / & the morning splits / in two // in one morning a janitor pushes slick red / across the tile floor / a color like dawn / that stains the sky for days // in the other / i am still sleeping / dreaming / of a cat yowling / trapped in a steel box / with no lock / & wondering how to get it out //

Drag

DRAG / adj. / marked by the wearing of clothing associated with the opposite sex; / [like] TRANSVESTITE / noun / a person [especially male] who assumes the dress & manner of the opposite sex // identity first defined / as the art of disguise it was never considered that this / was the art of escape / slipping out of our born gender / like handcuffs // the term TRANSGENDER / [adj.] / was not coined until 1965 / in a journal of pathology // our existence first named fetish / & then disease //

DRAG / verb / to be drawn or hauled along / to trail [like a body] on the ground // it's funny how one word / can mean two very different things / but not funny funny / more ironic / like drowning on dry land // its funny / [but not funny funny] how gay & drag are tied so tightly together / like wrists / & most people act like gay & queer / are the same damn thing / like the rest of us are / just here to hold the flag up // like we've never faced violence / for wearing the wrong clothes / or the right clothes / on the wrong bodies / or just having the wrong bodies // or being in the wrong place at the wrong time [where the place is anywhere / the time any time] //

in 2011 Marcal Camero Tye / was found dead in Forrest City, Arkansas / [a city with so many white hoods / flowing through its veins / that you can see the crosses burning / on people's tongues when they speak its name] // her life / punctuated by gunshots / her body dragged / beneath a car // but when the news report came in / she was called a man / in women's clothes // she was called a ghost / that left no body behind // despite law enforcement's best efforts / her killers were never found // & isn't it funny / [but not funny funny] / how one word can leave our mouth / twice / & only once does it taste like blood?

Gender of the Day

a paper doll
        every inch / of this body
     a scissor wound / that does not bleed

& the floor is covered
            in scraps of me

a dozen paper bodies
    trying   to   unfold /
                                into something new

      a body / where i feel / like i belong

Three Queers in a Car in America

it's Thanksgiving 2015 / & the sun glares sharp through the windows / the car shaking / & i do not know if it is from the roughness of the road or the speakers rattling / [like tin-cup change] / Weeknd singing over the bass / Robert shouting over both //

& i drive / like we breathe / [three queers in a car in America] / like he sings / *i'm a young god* / reckless / [like this is somewhere we belong] //

our car bounces tarmac / like drumstick rebounds snare / like sneakers kick blacktop / [while its down] / & the tires gasp / as i slide onto Crenshaw / & Robert shouts / "slow down / people like us don't survive traffic stops" / [& he sings] //

my god white / [in America] / & Robert's brown skin / seems to darken with fear / & i remember just who we are / all queer / most trans / all wrong / [& he sings] / *he get me redder than the devil* /
& i am
reminded how our bodies look on concrete / devil red / crimson tails leading into the gutter / & away / & i keep thinking /
'til i go nauseous //

& we are all so nauseous / so we do the only sane thing / & make it into a joke / [kinda humor too dark / to survive here] / laughing about / who dies first / of three queer bodies / palms up to the sky / when one is the color / of California dust / the others / clouds // when one boy struggles to undress girl / from other people's tongues / & i am still wearing man / like ill-fitting clothes //

& we all know that i will be the first / to live / & the last to die / because i look most like / the people behind the guns / & we are all wondering / how often we swallow this fear / whole / [& he answers] / *often / often* //

& we drive on slowly / careful / quiet / [as three queers in a car in America] / brake lights flashing / devil red / & we do not speak of death [& he sings] / *the night's almost up* / & we do not speak / *the night's almost done...* //

The House of Walls

prologue.
riddle: how many warning shots / can a body hold //
answer: how many shots can you take? //
the car shrieked like a wounded duck / half stuffed
with bird-shot / before my father snapped it's neck / before we picked
the pellets from our teeth // sirens spread their wings
of light / across the night sky / singing out their two note song //
riddle: how much is too much? //
answer: the cuffs close like teeth / around your wrists //

I.
the jail walls are as white / as the corpses / of trees
in a field of ash / the cleanest part of this place // concrete stained &
crusted / with dirt & piss & the red clay /
of bleach mingled blood // & the walls are a tapestry of black fingers
& palms / like frostbitten bodies buried in the snow / tar stain dark
from fingerprint dust / like hands pushing in from all around me / the
room's walls pressing in // i am huddled in the center of an empty cell
shivering from the cold / light
pouring in like counterfeit day / & i can hear them
through the tapestry walls / like you hear rain falling /
from inside your house / or waves striking the ship's hull
like fists / & i imagine that even Noah would have dreamt
of drowning //

II.
jeering & laughter echoes down the hall / & as hard as i try /
i can't make myself hate this man // a person pushes a hyena that deep
into their throat / you will forget it is there until
they laugh // if a person is forced to swallow the crows /
that make carrion out of him / even they will forget where
the cackling comes from // caged dog snarls at the steel when
teeth can't find skin / but both bring blood rushing to the surface
both are violence // *you seen*

him / my jugular tightens

under needlepoint teeth / *the faggot in cell* 6C? // solitary //
& his bark cuts concrete / makes splinters of bulletproof glass / echoes
off the walls like / you know why you're in here alone // like / you
know what happens to people like you / in here / so enjoy this silence
pooling / like blood / in the corners of floor //

    III.
my mouth is filled with dry dirt / tongue cracked like summer
farm land / breath heavy with my body's dust // in this place / where
times hands have been broken / off at the wrist / i cannot tell if it has
been minutes / or days // only that my cries / for water / have been
met with gun barrel eyes / & men barking / like fighting dogs // my
throat closed / like a fist around
itself / & is this not all / they ever wanted from me? // you wrap the
right kind of chain / around a dog's neck / it will choke itself to be free
am i not just another dog / barking at the walls /
howling at bleach white concrete / dreaming it is the moon //

    epilogue.
the cell door gapes open / like a broken jawed mouth /
this house of walls echoes / with the gnashing sound of steel teeth // i
limp down the hallways of this place / twisting like words / on justice's
crooked tongue / my heel dragging canyons in concrete dust // i take
my things from a silent man / voice torn scarlet & twitching / from his
throat // leave my glasses still in the bag / afraid to see the shredded
paper ghosts / trapped among these metal teeth // i step blind into the
light / of a different country / than the one i thought i left behind //

    riddle: a crippled queer limps / out of a jail in America /
        & into the throat / of the sun // what shape
        has their body been chewed into? //

    answer: whatever shape /
                the chalk line chooses //

To the People Who Call Me Brave

how do i explain
that there is no bravery in running
from a house on fire.
that this story begins with body
born boy
like animal skinning itself in reverse
& sewing itself up wrong.
that dressing like this feels less
like dressing up & more like dressing
a wound.
after slipping boy from my body
i am a burn victim
trying to grow a second skin
& this is not bravery
it is survival
it is trading fire
for firing squad
& declaring my body
bulletproof.
when you train the shotgun
of a mouth
on a body that you say cannot exist
i have already begun to fade
away
& your bullets pass through me
like ghosts.

Jaz Told Me to Write a Poem About the Things I Fear Putting into Words

for Taylor Flynn & Jaz Sufi

sometimes i fear that i cannot write a poem i have not named, so i tried for days to speak my fears into shape, each time i failed, & these are my failure's names:

On Bodies *or* i cannot believe in a god who would not give him the body he deserved.

On God *or* How to write an excuse with only three letters.

On Transphobia *or* Using proper pronouns is not fucking optional.

On Proper Pronouns *or* How i am willing to get arrested for assault over a one letter difference.

Telling the Difference *or* Loving this boy does not make him any less of a man.

On Homophobia *or* Our love was never meant to be a declaration of war.

On Homophobia *or* What exactly are you afraid of?

On Heterophobia *or* Why the fuck is this word not in the dictionary?

On Heterophobia *or* Yes, it is a legitimate fear, i should never have to hold someone's hand this tightly.

Holding Hands in Public *or* i am afraid of the red stains they make of these queer bodies.

These Queer Bodies *or* This soft flesh was never intended to become a holder for stray fists or knives.

On Knives *or* The way we have made a game of hiding them from each other when we have been drinking.

When We Have Been Drinking *or* All of the edges grow sharper when the sun begins to set.

Sharp Edges *or* How these soft bodies became eulogies of this blood escaping.

On Blood *or* How i never told you how close i came to suicide when i said that there was too much blood in my body & it needed to escape— you already knew.

On Suicide *or* There is no forgiveness or salvation in this death.

On Death *or* Between them & us i do not know who will kill us first

*On the Midnight Sky, Fireworks Calling to Us
Like a Mother in the Distance*

53 dead / queer bodies spread across the night
club floor / a host of heartbeats with bullet wounds /
guilty of nothing / but surviving / that long //

& they say that this wouldn't have happened /
if they had been strapping / like a young kid
in the hood's never been shot for strapping / never
died because they had a gun / or *it looked like
a gun* / in his hand / or he had hands at all //

like the winter after Trayvon died / mothers didn't
stop buying their sons black hoodies / like we ain't
all learning to be afraid of the dark / behind our eyelids //

& the summer after that / Tim & i stood /
backs to brick walls / faces to the hot black silk /
of an 80 degree California night / scarlet sunrise
beginning / to drip from the horizon //

talking about funerals / & how growing up
black / or queer / you watch your mother
beginning to bury you / over the evening news /
& maybe then i didn't understand / how easy he
could look at the back of his hand / & mistake it
for the night sky //

but now, i want to call him / tell him i am afraid to
dance / [& not like we / ain't always been / but
not like that] // tell him that i think i understand /
disappearing / into the night / or a crowd / anything
that will take us //

tell him / ain't it funny / how we dance with our hands
up / like we can reach god / [like we still believe /
he's up there] / like we ain't guilty of anything / but
survival / like we got hands at all //

i wanna say / how you breathe / on the 4th of July? /
when it sounds like the sky is screaming / for us
to return to it / when fireworks sound / like gunshots /
like mother's voices / like *child, please come home* //
i wanna say / remember when we weren't afraid? /
when we didn't feel like / paper targets? / didn't watch
the news / start counting bullets / & graves /
wondering when the body count's gonna be high enough /
[or if it ever will] //

i want to say all of this / message him / near midnight /
like we can only speak / of this / when the sky has
made itself into a grave //

i want to tell him / that i feel myself becoming an exit
wound / before they even pull the trigger //

Panic Attack as A Four-Part Word Problem

after Nicole Paoli

I. The average person can bite down with a force of 171 lbs. Human teeth achieve a rating of 5/10 on the Hohs Scale of Mineral Hardness, equal to shark's teeth & stronger than steel. The steel plating on the hull of the titanic was nearly ¾ of an inch thick. How many hours a day does the anxiety crash over you like waves? Insert this number as X, & solve for the number of shipwrecks your teeth have carved onto the inside of your cheek.

II. A set of healthy lungs can hold 5 liters of oxygen. The average breath is one tenth of this. They call this the tidal volume [as though our chests were oceans, filled with waves]. When the body begins hyperventilating this number is cut in half, & oxygen is rapidly replaced with CO_2. Assuming that you started hyperventilating three minutes ago, how long have you felt like you were drowning? & how long until you actually do?

III. At rest, the human heart beats 60-100 times per minute [steady as a military drum], but during a heart attack the rhythm can well exceed this [tachycardia turns the heart's drum to blast beat]. If a 6ft. wave takes 15 seconds to reach the shore, it is moving at 17.5 mph, & if blood moves through the body at a speed of less than 1 mph, then the chest must be an ocean filled with waves. Blood could not possibly move so slow. Assuming that it feels as though the waves of blood crashing in your heart will break through the levees of your chest, solve for the chance that this is a heart attack. Solve for how long the phone call with the paramedics will last. Solve for how long it will take the ambulance to arrive.

IV. Given that your chest is an ocean, & the waves are moving at 17.5 mph, & that the tides of your breath are now as shallow as a graveyard of ships, & the ambulance is on the way, & the CO_2 is trickling like water into your lungs, & your teeth are gritted around the hull of your mouth, assume that your vision is beginning to swim, salt water filling your eyes, assume that you are slipping under the waves, assume you have never been good at treading water. Will you still be conscious when the ambulance arrives?

Gender of the Day

the y-incision in a chest

when you take person & peel back living,
        what remains?

when you peel body of man
        or woman,
        what remains?

when i end up here / & they peel me /
  like overripe fruit
      what will remain?

    except for a body,
    wrong gender noosed to the tag
    on its toe.

Unfinished Scenes

scene:
i am dancing in an empty room / cane discarded / body
swaying like a ship / mid capsize // my right leg / vibrato / panicked
violin shaking / under my body's weight / shifting
from stiletto'd foot / to foot / percussion to the beat /
of an empty song

scene:
i slip the knife under my ribs / like a secret / folded into a note //
my stomach peels back like paper / inside are 100 cocoons /
body bags / sewn from silk / for bodies / just like mine

scene:
a child runs / bare feet slapping linoleum / velvet dress trailing / violet
wind behind him / his mother smiles / unaware
hands him a shawl / of pale silk // he wraps it tight / around his
slender frame & begins to unwind

scene:
imagine that body is metal / taking shape
that father / & bully / & mouth / are blacksmith / hammering body /
into boy // folding bad blood / & loathing / layers deep
& then when the body cracks / discarding the shards

scene:
100 butterflies bloom / from my open guts / their crooked wings
beat / percussion into the empty air // the coroner laughs / tells their
assistant about these twisted things / *[gynandromorphic butterflies]* says
that through some mistake / or miracle / their bodies unwind /
in the cocoon / & sew themselves into something new / not male
not female / but both / & neither // how so many things in nature
stitch themselves / into a shape that we call wrong // butterfly /
moth / lobster / cardinal / [feathers & shells like snow
stained with blood] // the assistant snatches one by the curve
of its smaller / female wing / pushes a fishhook through its chest /
& hangs it from my pale violet toe

scene:
child emerges / years later
wrapped in strands of silk / arrowhead emerging
from inside the cocoon / crooked shards
not boy / not girl / but both /
    & neither

Calloused Hands

i have never felt soft enough
to be woman,
skin like chisel cut wood.

femininity has never fit me quite right,
like i'm always trying to wear the wrong size,
always pulling stitches at the seams.

see i've got shoulders like mountainsides,
ribcage like a barrel even when the slats break.
i've got fists like small-town America

which is to say they never look broke
    until you get too close
           & callouses run all through me.

i have always been more broken nail & burst vein
than manicure & daisy chain,
& dressing the way i want has always felt
like forcing a GI Joe into Barbie clothes.

i have never felt soft enough to be
half the woman that i want to be,
but i guess my mother never taught me

        woman like that.

she taught me woman like a turtle carrying it's home
on its back, across three state lines.

woman like elbow grease & bust knuckles

but a hammer in hand,

like coffee mug shrapnel
& three separations,

like holding this family together till
her teeth were skinned & bleeding.

taught me mother like a brick
through a basement window
& a bed of broken glass,
but *we're not sleeping in the cold tonight.*

taught me woman means whatever means necessary.
taught me woman means violent when she needs to be,
there's a reason stilettos stole their name
                                             from a knife.

taught me sometimes survival ain't for the fittest,
just those who are willing to survive.

taught me woman is surviving.
taught me woman is not a place you reach
without a few scars to your name.

                        we both have so many scars.

   so when i told her that i—*he*—had become *they*,
that i had murdered her son while she was looking away,
she took me by the hand,
               told me that she wouldn't always
   remember, that she was sorry,
   that had been her son for so long,

& then, maybe for the first time,
   i really felt like a woman.
       her hand in mine,
          no longer her son,

feeling the callouses that run all through us.

When My Partner Writes

a love poem / for someone other than me / i read it as slow as my eyes will carry me / my pupils black gullets / swallowing every word / & i fall in love with them all over again

//

it's something in the way they writes / about his cheek / the skin his razor neglects / stubble collecting as if it were dust / the soft way they speak of his body / this warm animal they curl their body around / in the deep breaths of the night / ice crystals forming in the window fog / so much like the way their body cradles mine

//

it is in the way they write about his eyes / as though they were such simple things / as though you could not dedicate entire manuscripts / to a lover's single blink / they speak his eyes into granite / & for a moment i am half in love with the soft stone of this man

//

this poem reminds me that there are nesting dolls / in all our hearts / that if you love deeply enough / they just keep opening / if you truly love / you can always fit more people inside

Gender of the Day

an unstained / & unbitten / tongue
        that has never tasted   its own blood
      that does not drip with apology
              like sweet liquored hurt.

a bloodless tongue / cloaked in teeth /
      that billow in the wind   of my jaw

                                    into a wide open
              grin.

Aubade [From Body to Little Black Dress]

   how soon the sun
   breaks the indigo nails of dawn
   & lazily spreads across clouds
   like razor-cut blood into bathroom sink,

& birds are singing   what sounds like goodbye

      or goodnight

   but the notes are all wrong.

they danced as close as lovers might
   separated by only whiskey sweat

    wearing each other like skin.

tasting each move,

       each breath,

 whole bodies
      as tongues.

but just as sun must rise,
  dress descends

       across the floor
     like a crumpled accordion
        of night.

body remains [feeling all the irony
   in this word]
 butcher paper thin
       & pale,
 all too boy
standing over their second skin,
coiled black snake shed & burning.

inside a single lipstick stain

bloody as a beating heart

                                                      left behind

          a goodnight kiss
          ember still hot
            to the touch.

If / Then or An Open Letter to High School GSAs

"⊃" represents an if/then statement in symbolic logic, the words preceding it being the "if" those after being the "then."

i am sitting in a room dripping rainbows
from the ceiling like blood or milk & i
do not feel like i belong ⊃ maybe there
just isn't enough glitter in my blood

[&] i am sitting in this room wondering
if i'm really "queer enough" ⊃ maybe
this is another theft i was never taught
to prepare for

i open my mouth to speak & nothing
comes out ⊃ ask yourself, whose
voice put shackles on this tongue

[was it yours?]

i am in a safe-space & i am afraid
of offending a cis-het ally stitching
their tragedy hungry lips to our
all too bloody skin ⊃ this "safe-
space" learned everything it knows
from handcuffs

[&] i [queer-queen / rainbow
warrior sprouting butterfly
knife wings] am sitting in this
room being judged for the
glitter content of my un-giftable
blood ⊃ what about the kids with
closets nailed to the inside of
their skin? the boys sewn from
bruises sprouting from their
fathers' fists? the genderqueer
kids who can't afford hair dye

or $60 slogan tee shirts?

[when did this become a popularity contest?
another kind of heaven that will never let us in?]

they're not counted $\supset$
count me out

Ode to Laura Jane Grace, Ending in a Fistful of Ash

after Hanif Willis-Abdurraqib

& the ocean strikes the rocks / like a heaven of fists / & recedes /
crashes like a broken cymbal / on the shore / & takes
a little piece of the earth with it / & ain't that just like the stage? //
which is to say / crowd swells up at your feet / they always
swallow something / take a piece of you home // & ain't we so used
to leaving a part of us behind / sweat / or blood / or any part of us /
that holds enough salt / to mistake itself for the sea //

//

when a person dies we say that they have passed *on*,
left this world behind. & when we walk down the street
& no one sees our face as a re-bound book,
we call this passing.
as though there is only one word's distance
between life & death for people like us.
& we both remember how a cop's hands close
like curtains over our bodies like a stage.
how our skin learned sunset & midnight only
in how our blood abandoned it.
i know you remember every dark room like the back
of another person's hand, still remember
how the first dress felt—like skin.
felt like stepping into your own body
for the first time.
felt like resurrection.

//

i cup my name in the hollow curve of my mouth / & how lucky
to be given / a name that has never ached / to burn // that does not
taste of bitten tongues / that can be so easily mistaken / for a body /
you are trying to escape // & is a flame not something / like a prayer /
& is a prayer not something / to sit heavy on the tongue / before it is
given flight / & is paper so unlike a bird / when folded right? // may

15th / you cupped your name in the hollow curve of your hand / &
watched it burn / letters curling back over themselves /
like a body / trying to shed its skin // & is a flame not
something / holy / when taught the right way to burn / & is paper not
something / like a prayer in the way it surrenders / to an open flame /
& is our body not something / like a fire / we pass through / & never
arrive //

    it is something like a prayer / to take the name you were given /
    & let it pass through your fingers / as soft feathers of ash //

Gender of the Day

a feather

    falling   upwards
        into the sky

twisting on the wind / lost child /
    returning to wing / tasting the sky /
drinking in the bent fifth note of the light

clouds like blooming flowers / of salt & dust /
    exploding dandelions the color of an egg shell /
cracking backwards / the shape of shards /
    becoming whole

The Principle of Explosion

$$\forall X : (Y \wedge \neg Y) \Rightarrow X$$
from a falsehood anything follows

for the sake of argument / let us assume that i am a boy / & not a boy / that i am just as girl / as i am not girl // i am so accustomed to being defined by everything i am not //

crushed between self-doubt & expectations / for what this body can or should be // as though the metal of my skin has been molded / into a Janus coin / & no matter which side i call / i am always coming up wrong //

but there is a line where i both exist / & unexist / where this body becomes detonation // [which is to say / in the moment when i become impossible / i become a singularity] //

my entire existence becomes / event horizon / a single point of light expanding // like the heat from the big bang created the possibility / of everything //

from a falsehood / follows anything / which is to say / if i both can / & cannot be / there is a case /
that i am //

about torrin a. greathouse

torrin a. greathouse is a genderqueer trans womxn & cripple-punk from Southern California. She is the Editor-in-Chief of Black Napkin Press. Their work is published/forthcoming in *Bettering American Poetry, The Offing, BOAAT, Apogee, Tinderbox, Frontier, Lunch Ticket, Assaracus,* & *Glass: A Journal of Poetry*. She is a *Best of Net, Best New Poets,* & *Pushcart Prize* nominee. When they are not writing, their hobbies include pursuing a bachelor's degree, awkwardly drinking coffee at parties, & trying to find some goddamn size 13 heels.

Made in the USA
Coppell, TX
10 May 2021